Heart Talking

Inspiring Poems for the Soul

Steve Raggio

Blue Sky Publishing

Copyright © 2025 by Steve Raggio

All rights reserved.

No portion of this book may be reproduced in any form without written permission from the publisher or author, except as permitted by U.S. copyright law.

Contents

Preface — XI

1. God and the Soul — 1

    God is All

    Our Savior

    Baby Jesus

    Christmas

    God's Painting

    I Am Not Worthy

    Sweet Jesus I Pray to Thee

    God is Good

    A New Kind of Love

    Grace

    I Pray

    Dear Lord

    God is the Driver

    It's Not Your Plan

    His Birth

    Cast Your Worries

Lord Guide Me

Your Soul

The Ray of Light

My Dear Lord

I Pray

Forgive

He Died

We Say the Prayer

God Knows My Heart

You Don't Know

Pray

He Shed His Blood

Mary

We Don't Know

Heaven

God Knows

Grace

He is Risen

Peace

Thank You, Lord

Value

Life

Joy

The World

Enjoy

2. Values of the Soul   46

   You Give
   A Gentle Calm
   You Don't Know
   It's Hard to See
   Don't Let Your Past
   The Joy
   Guidance
   Your Way
   Rain
   Good Morning
   A Beautiful Day
   My Heart is Big
   God Puts
   A Teacher is Special
   I'm Sorry
   A New Year is Coming
   Enjoy Where You're At
   Loss
   We Seek
   This World
   Your Truth
   Be Yourself
   Your Heart
   Life is Hard
   Life is Hard

Time

Humble

Healing

Calling

Sunrise

Appreciate

Sight

Your Worth

Your Walk

Words

I Gave My All

A Kind Word

We All Live

Heartbreak

Smile

You Tried

Love Life

I Love Pictures

Judge Me

Give Thanks

I'm Not Perfect

Peace

Wisdom

Have Compassion

A Lie

Love

I'm Going

A New Year

Sometime

I Don't Know

Be a Beacon

Negativity

Friends

I Search

Friends are Special

I Don't Know

I Have Hurt

I Live My Life

I Don't Know the Why

I Look For Clarity

You Give Your All

I'm Trying

The Birds

You May Like Me

Disrespect

I Want a Love

My Heart is Heavy

I'm Searching

A New Day

Disrespect II

Trust

You May Be

In This Life
A Beautiful Day
Memorial Day
Take It Slow
The Sun is Rising
I Don't Know Why
Cherish Your Loved Ones
I'm Not Perfect
Cancer
A Beautiful Morning
Give Your Love
I Sit Here and Ponder
Look For the Good
I May Live
The Beauty
The Path

3. Family and Friends and the Soul   144
Brady Charles
Gabby
Miss Lauren
Allie Girl
My Dad
My Mom
My Brother
My Sister

My Brother Nerv

I Lost a Bud

My Friend

(Garrett O'Connor)

Audra

Savanna

Pinball Junkies

The River Rats

Big Cliff

They Call Me Bruce

Shakey Loves His Traeger

Terapy Girl Terapy Boy

Teddy and Scottie

Addison and Maddison

A Great Group

TD and Stitch

My Friend Mason

Tejas Vaqueros

The Blessings of a Child

The Joy

Big Nasty

My Buddy Gil

Brothers Guidry

My Bud

Acknowledgements   178

About the Author 179

Preface

I hope these poems provide some inspiration to the reader as it did for me through writing them. Healing from divorce or a breakup can take time. But through God blessing me with these poems that came into my head, it gave me an avenue to help with the process. If I can inspire one reader to be a better self and get closer to God, that brings me joy! I don't claim to be acclaimed but I hope you enjoy these poems from my heart!

One

God and the Soul

God is All

God is my refuge
God is my light.
He makes things clear
He makes things bright.
He shows me the path
and clears me the way,
so that I can handle
each and every day.
I may stumble
and I may fall
but he's there to catch me
through it all.
So don't rely on you
and I won't on me.
Rely on him
so that you can see.

***

Our Savior

Our Savior was born
on this glorious day.
We celebrate his birth
as we share and we pray.
So celebrate your loved ones
while they're here on this earth.
God gave them to us
since the day of their birth.
Some will die early
and some will die late,
but trust in our Savior
for our final fate.
This earth is just a place
to enjoy while we're here.
To love others
and hold them near.
The ultimate journey
is through the clouds up above.
Where God will show us his abundant
love.

***

Baby Jesus

Baby Jesus,
born in a manger,
what a glorious sight.
On a beautiful starlit night.
Came into this world
to endure struggles and pain.
To follow God's path
for our ultimate gain.
It's plain to see
he died for you,
and he died for me.
So accept this gift,
we may stumble,
and we may fall.
But his Christmas gift
is the best of all!

***

Christmas

Christmas,
It's not just presents, green, red, and a tree.
It's me caring about you,
and you about me.
It's giving thanks
for his glorious birth.
To show us his love,
and give us our worth.
Our worth is a blessing
God gives from above.
Through baby Jesus
With all of his love!

***

God's Painting

God's painting is bright,
sometimes it's sun,
sometimes it's snow
and sometimes it's light.
A canvas to see
blessings from above.
Take it all in,
he's showing his love.
All the beauty from nature
he gives us each day.
So give him thanks
as we kneel and we pray.
Snow may keep us in,
sun may bring us out.
But God's painting
we can't live without!

***

I Am Not Worthy

I am not worthy
but please make me see
my purpose in life
that you wrote for me.
The path that I take
with you by my side
your unconditional love
in you I confide.
I tried it my way,
I stumbled and fell.
But you picked me up
and you made me well.
I know I'm not perfect
but with your amazing grace,
show me the way Lord
until I see your face!

***

STEVE RAGGIO

Sweet Jesus I Pray to Thee

That you will come down and bless my family.
I know I haven't always done things right.
But please forgive me with all your might.
We have this virus, it's everywhere you see.
I pray that it will leave us, just let us be.
I know we need to change our ways.
More love and compassion throughout these days.
Less anger, less jealousy, less sin and less greed.
Bring us back to you, the true thing that we need.
So I ask you to bless us, and make us see.
That it's not about us, and it's not about me.

***

God is Good

God is good
every single day.
He loves us dearly,
as we listen and we pray.
Let his voice
speak to your heart.
Create a new beginning,
make a new start.
A start with compassion,
a start with love,
for those around you
and God up above.
Let peace flow
into your soul,
and love for others
will be your ultimate goal!

***

STEVE RAGGIO

A New Kind of Love

I pray to you Jesus,
my Lord above,
that you will shower me
with all your love.
I know I don't deserve it,
a sinner is me,
but I know my repentance
brings me closer to thee.
I ask that you bless me,
with a new kind of love.
That when I share it,
it comes from above.
I know you suffered
died and now live,
fill me with the love
that I can abundantly give.
So I close this poem
with thanks to thee,
because most of all
you died for me.

***

Grace

God is good
God is all.
You may stumble
or you may fall.
He will pick you up
and show you the way.
His grace is amazing
each and every day.
Give him the wheel
to steer you clear
of the storm of life
and do not fear.
For if you let him
take you on that ride.
He will show you grace
and be by your side.

***

I Pray

I pray for you
I pray for me.
I pray for those
who cannot see.
I pray for peace
for comfort and joy.
I pray for the girl
I pray for the boy.
The baby to come
the mom and the dad.
The joy in their hearts,
happy or sad.
I pray for the soldier
who keeps us free.
So you can be you
and I can be me.
It's very simple,
if we all would just pray
for peace in this world
and have a good day!

***

Dear Lord

Dear Lord, I pray to thee,
that you guide me,
protect me,
watch over my family.
Dear Lord, we are weak,
you are strong,
keep us faithful
all day and all night long.
Take away the hurt,
replace it with glad,
show us your mercy
erase all the sad.
Thank you for blessings
you send us each day,
may we appreciate them,
as we kneel and we pray!

***

God is the Driver

God is the driver,
enjoy the ride.
If you just have faith,
he will be by your side.
The road may be rough
with bridges to cross,
just let him drive;
don't worry
He's the boss.
The journey is simple,
don't try to take the wheel,
let the boss drive,
in the end you will heal!

***

It's Not Your Plan

It's not your plan,
you think it is.
It's not your place,
it's always his.
He's here for you,
just open your heart.
Start a new day,
make a new start.
Give him the glory,
he will be by your side
to guide your path,
to show you the ride.
The ride is simple
it's tried and it's true.
Let him drive
for me and for you!

***

STEVE RAGGIO

His Birth

His birth is special
A symbol of joy.
Jesus is here
for the girl and the boy.
He came for us all,
to show us the way,
to live and to love,
to start a new day.
Just trust in him,
and celebrate his birth,
his amazing grace
to show you your worth.
Your worth is special,
he gives you that too,
to share with others
and see what you can do!

***

Cast Your Worries

Cast your worries
God says it so.
It's in the book
for all to know.
We concentrate on worry,
with strife and with fear.
Material things are first,
God is in the rear.
Don't worry about
what's now and will be,
have faith in him
each day you will see.
His grace is for you
and his grace is for me!

***

Lord Guide Me

Lord guide me,
show me the way.
To start a new path,
to brighten someone's day.
Let me be a beacon,
a light that shines bright.
To illuminate the day
and brighten the night.
Lord guide me to love
for the few and the less.
To give it my all
and show you my best.
It's not what we give
it's give from the heart.
Lord guide me to give
to give from the start!

***

Your Soul

You soul is priceless,
cherish it with love.
A special gift,
from God up above.
Feed it with good
with truth and with right,
and blessings will flow
each day and each night.
Your soul is on a road
to travel with care,
to enjoy the ride,
to love and to share.
Value your soul,
his love and his grace,
until one day
we may see his face!

***

STEVE RAGGIO

The Ray of Light

The ray of light
that God shines bright.
Is here to see.
It's here for you and here for me.
Just open your eyes
and let it glow
into your heart
so all will know.
All will know
the light you shine
upon the hearts
of yours and mine,
so be the beacon
for all to see
your ray of light
for you and for me!

***

My Dear Lord

My dear Lord,
I contemplate struggles,
I contemplate pain;
I see my future
I see my shame
I ask for forgiveness
I beg for grace.
To feel your mercy,
to touch your face.
I don't deserve it,
I never will.
But I get a little closer
and stand more still.
The stillness is there
for all to embrace.
Until one day
I may see your face!
Amen!

***

I Pray

I pray for those,
for those in need,
for those lost
for God to intercede.
His grace is good,
it's here to stay
to live in your life
to start a new day.
I pray for peace,
for joy in your life,
no more hurt,
no more strife.
I pray that we see
what God has for you
and God has for me!

***

Forgive

Forgive those around you,
he says it in the prayer.
He also wants us
to love and to share.
Forgive your past
the pain and the hurt.
Start a new path
to value your worth.
Your worth is special
it says who you are,
to share with others
both near and afar.
So I ask for forgiveness
for guidance and grace.
Lord, show me the way
to your eternal place!

***

He Died

He died for me,
he died for you.
His blood poured out
for the many and the few.
To give his life
through torment and pain,
for us sinners
so we shall gain.
To gain the love
that he gave to all,
so when we stumble
we shall not fall.
His grace is awesome
his love is true.
Thank you Lord
for what you do!

***

We Say the Prayer

We say the prayer,
it's plain to see
what it means for you,
what it means for me.
Forgive others
as they forgive you,
love your enemies
as they should too.
It's not who's right
and not who's wrong,
it's a love for one another
so we all shall belong.
Belong to a purpose
that God puts in place,
for all to be united
in his special space!

***

Thank You God

Thank you God,
tor all that you are.
You created all things
both near and afar.
The wonders of the earth
for all to enjoy.
The blessing of birth
the girl and the boy.
The joy of the baby,
that beautiful smile.
It warms the heart
for more than a while.
Thanks for your love
and thanks for your grace.
It's more than enough
to put a smile on my face!

***

God Knows My Heart

God knows my heart,
he knows my truth.
Throughout my life
way back to my youth.
I made mistakes
along the way.
But he picked me up
and shows me the way.
The way is simple
it's tried and it's true.
Put your faith in him,
he will show you what to do!

***

STEVE RAGGIO

You Don't Know

You don't know the way,
you don't know the day.
You don't know the why,
you don't know the how.
God knows how long
our clock is to hit.
It may be a while
or just a little bit.
So live life here
with joy and with love,
until the time
he takes us above!

***

Pray

Pray for healing,
pray for well being,
pray for caring,
pray for sharing,
pray for love,
it comes from above.
Pray for peace
that wars may cease.
Pray for the sick
for healing and care.
Pray for compassion
that we all should share!

***

He Shed His Blood

He shed his blood for me,
that if I believe
and trust in him,
I will see.
I will see beauty,
I will see love,
the unconditional kind
that comes from above.
His grace is awesome
brings peace to the heart,
warms your soul
to make a fresh start.
His suffering was tough,
blood from the cross.
Makes me thankful
he cared for me enough!

***

Mary

Mary did you know,
that your son,
the leader of the show,
is watching the actors
who don't know where to go.
They don't know the path,
but he has the way.
He can show them
each and every day.
If they would just ask him
to be in the show.
He will tell them
exactly where to go.
The path is simple,
just ask Mary's son.
Please Jesus
I come to you
let your will be done!

***

We Don't Know

We don't know
the when or the why.
God takes a two-year-old girl,
God takes a two-year-old guy.
We question his motive,
we question his grace,
but we all have
doubt on our face.
We say,
"how could he take
someone so young,"
if you just look in the book
and follow his tongue,
you will know that
we are on a test run.
Life is temporary
on this place
we call earth,
it's written
since our birth.
Look to the sky
and give him your soul,
Heaven is real
it's your ultimate goal!

***

Heaven

Heaven,
we don't know the place,
we don't know the time.
Have never seen his face
but just a little faith
in what he went through
for me and for you,
should bring you
to what you should do.
Just ask him to help you
to be by your side,
it makes it easier
for this life we call the ride.
The ride is simple
it's tried and it's true,
give Him the reigns
and see what he can do!

***

Life is Precious

Life is precious
take it in stride.
We don't know how long
or bumpy the ride.
The ride is a journey,
with joy and with pain,
we will have sunshine
and we will have rain.
Take in the journey
and enjoy the ride,
look up to him
to be by your side.
Give him the wheel
to steer your clear,
to free you
from worry and fear!

***

God Knows

God knows your troubles,
he knows your past,
he knows what will
and what won't last.
He knows your truth,
he knows your way,
if only you trust him
each and every day.
Put your faith in him,
let him take the wheel,
good things will come
each day you will heal!

***

Grace

Grace is beautiful,
it comes from above
it warms your heart.
With his amazing love
it's there to receive,
it's free for all,
if you just believe
and not put up a wall.
So open your heart,
accept his grace
to soothe your soul
for a better place!

***

He is Risen

He is risen,
what a beautiful thing.
He forgives our sins
while the angels sing.
The tomb is open,
he's gone above,
to meet our maker
with abundant love.
Love for you,
and love for me,
if we just open our eyes
so we can see.
To see his glory
his compassion and all,
so we can be thankful
and we can stand tall.
Stand tall in his mercy,
stand tall in his grace,
until the day
we may see his face!

***

Peace

Peace is awesome,
a gift from above,
to warm your soul
to show God's love.
He gives you that peace
and shows you the way,
to love others
and make someone's day.
To make someone's day,
be kind and be giving,
show them you care
so they can start living.
Living a life
with compassion for all,
so they can have peace
and they can stand tall!
Peace is knowing
God lives in your heart,
so start a new day
and make a new start!

***

Thank You, Lord

Thank you, Lord,
tor this beautiful day.
The sun is shining,
it feels like May.
The birds are singing,
the trees are green,
the sky is blue
like I've never seen.
I'm truly thankful
I can breathe this air.
I have friends and family
that truly care.
So thanks to you
for your love and grace,
and let me live
in this wonderful place!

***

Value

Each life has value,
it's plain to see.
Some are more humble
than you are than me.
It's not about the money,
it's not about the fame,
it's not about the status
it's not about the game.
The value is simple,
we fail to see,
it's not about you
and it's not about me.
Value those around you
and show them your love.
Show that you care
for what's up above.
It's there for you,
though you stumble and fall.
The value is grace,
for one and for all!

***

Life

Life is like a ride
taken on a bus.
You can enjoy the sights
or sit around and fuss.
You can see the beauty
of the birds and the trees.
Take in the journey
and enjoy the breeze.
You can sit around and mope,
negativity and all.
Won't do any good,
In the end you will fall.
So make your choice,
God gives you that too.
Life a full life,
and love all the way through!

***

Joy

Joy is a product
from God up above.
You get it when you focus
on his grace and his love.
Joy is special,
it soothes your heart,
comforts your soul,
creates a new start.
A start to a new day
what adventures it brings,
the sweet sounds
when the angel sings.
Sing the joyful sound
with glory and praise,
thanking him
until our final days!

***

The World

The world is in chaos,
it's plain to see.
People don't care
about you or about me.
Selfish and greed
have taken its toll.
People are angry
and many are cold.
Not cold by degrees,
but cold in the heart.
If only they could awaken
and make a new start.
Start by giving
to someone in need.
If it's just a kind word
or it's a good deed.
If we don't turn to God,
with all of his grace,
this world will grieve
and never see his face!

***

STEVE RAGGIO

Enjoy

Enjoy your blessings,
your time on earth,
what God has given you
since your day of birth.
Enjoy the simple things,
the things that really matter,
the things that are coming
and not the latter.
Enjoy the beauty
of the ocean and sky,
a beautiful sunset,
a hot apple pie.
Enjoy your family,
your kids and your wife,
enjoy your siblings
your time and your life.
It may be short
or it may be long,
so enjoy your time
until you are gone.

***

HEART TALKING

Two

Values of the Soul

You Give

You give
and you don't get,
you give and you want to quit .
But don't quit ,
because someone
has your back
even if you're under attack.
He's looking down
and sees all,
picks you up
when you fall.
So don't worry
if someone fails
to see your worth,
God has you
since the day of your birth!

***

STEVE RAGGIO

A Gentle Calm

A gentle calm,
a cool breeze,
you feel it
as it passes through the trees.
The sun has come
to brighten your day,
to shed light
as you make your way.
Start your path
to touch someone's heart.
Bring joy to their life,
so they can make a new start.
A start with giving,
a start with sharing,
a start with loving,
a start with caring.
So enjoy the calm
of this beautiful day,
and thank him
as we reflect and we pray!

***

You Don't Know

You don't know the pain
that's in someone's heart.
You don't know the journey
they took from the start.
You don't know the struggles
they have in their life.
You don't know their joy,
you don't know their strife.
So live with compassion,
with love for all,
so they may not stumble
and they can stand tall!

***

It's Hard to See

It's hard to see people hurting,
not happy, no glee.
Christmas should bring
a smile to your face,
but some are struggling
and don't know their place.
God guide me
to show me someone
and bless them with care,
with love and compassion
that I know I should share.
Show me the way
to bless them with love,
and they can give thanks
to you up above!

***

Don't Let Your Past

Don't let your past
define yourself.
Don't let your past
put feelings on the shelf.
You know who you are,
you know what you give.
Show your love
and truly live.
Live for the moment,
live for the joy,
live for your loved ones,
the girl and the boy.
It's a short time
we have in this place,
so live it with kindness
and a smile on your face!

***

The Joy

The joy of a child,
a beautiful thing.
Their love is pure,
the comfort that they bring.
Those little words
they speak each day,
bring a smile to your face
in every way.
Their joy is a blessing
from God up above,
he shows us that
through a child's love!

***

Guidance

I need guidance,
from God up above,
to show me the way
to peace and his love.
His love is pure,
his abundant grace,
please show me the way
and show me the place.
The place you want me
and the path that I take,
to show me wisdom
and not a mistake.
I want your will,
I need your grace,
to bring joy
and a smile to my face!

***

Your Way

You can do it your way
or you can do it his.
It's really a choice,
to hit or to miss.
To hit is his will,
to miss is yours.
His will creates joy,
yours closes doors.
'My will be done,'
it says in the book,
he teaches us wisdom
if only we look.
His wisdom is pure,
his love and his grace,
will surely put
a smile on your face!

***

Rain

Rain will come,
rain will go,
what comes next
we don't know.
We may walk,
we may run,
enjoy the day,
let's have fun!

***

STEVE RAGGIO

Good Morning

May your day be guided
by God's love and his grace,
to show you the way
and put a smile on your face!
Good morning to thanks,
good morning to love,
good morning to others
and God up above.
It's a good morning
to be thankful and kind,
to leave anger
and animosity behind!

***

A Beautiful Day

A beautiful day,
be thankful for that,
always a blessing
wherever you're at.
Go for a walk,
take in a ride,
spend it with loved ones,
right by your side.
It's the simple things
that bring us a smile
so live for the moment
and live for the while!

***

STEVE RAGGIO

My Heart is Big

My heart is big
and I give it all,
but if you accept it
don't let me fall.
I will pick you up
and be by your side,
through the whole journey
on every ride.
I will be your best friend
your ride or die,
your love and shoulder
when you need to cry.
But please don't break it,
cause you might not find,
a heart this big,
a heart like mine!

***

God Puts

God puts someone in your life,
may be a girlfriend,
may be a husband,
may be a wife.
May be a short time,
may be very long,
may create a rhyme,
may create a song.
If that someone
brings you joy,
cherish it
like a child with a toy.
We don't know the beginning
and we don't know the end,
but to be happy and loved
is what God would truly send!

***

STEVE RAGGIO

A Teacher is Special

A teacher is special,
our kids in their way,
giving them guidance
as they start each day.
Their journey is special,
each step that they take.
A teacher is there,
for the good
and their mistake.
But mistakes will happen,
each day they will fall.
The teacher picks them up
and makes them stand tall!
So thank a teacher
for all that they do,
to guide our kids
for me and for you!

***

I'm Sorry

I'm sorry if I hurt you
I'm sorry if I failed.
I'm sorry if I'm gone
and the boat just sailed.
Life is a journey,
only God knows the way.
I hope he guides me
each and every day.
My path may be crooked,
my path may be straight,
but if I steer off course
please do not hate.
My goal is simple,
for me to stand tall,
not to just love one
but for me to love all!

***

STEVE RAGGIO

A New Year is Coming

A new year is coming
for all to embrace,
to bring joy to life
and a smile on someone's face.
Take on the new year
with a renewed mind,
with more love for others,
more compassion and kind.
Kindness is simple,
doesn't cost you a thing,
let's show it more
in the new year we bring!

***

Enjoy Where You're At

Enjoy where you're at,
breathe in the air,
give someone a hug,
show them you care.
It's the little things
that should mean a lot;
a child's first word,
their smile on the spot.
Listen to the birds,
the stream's soothing sound.
Give thanks that you're here
because some are not around.
Most of all,
give thanks to God up above,
his mercy and grace,
his forgiveness and love!

***

Loss

We lose a loved one,
a sibling or a spouse.
We may lose our dog
or even lose our house.
But through it all
if only we see,
it's not about you
and it's not about me.
God has a plan,
it may be short
or may be long.
You don't know your story
and you don't know how long.
So live your life
with compassion and love,
for those around you
and him up above.

***

We Seek

We seek for validation,
we seek for the game.
We seek approval,
for love and not shame.
We seek for eternal,
where we hope that we go.
But when the end comes,
we do not know.
We seek for love,
for kindness,
for peace,
from God up above.
If only we seek
what he freely gives,
his love and grace
and how he truly lives.
He lives in your heart,
if you let it be.
Just allow it
and you will see,
the blessings are there
for you and for me!

***

This World

This world is twisted,
it's broken and lost.
Won't get back to morals
at any cost.
It's written in the book,
these things will come to pass.
There will be strife
and good will not last.
The bad days are coming,
but hold your head high.
Keep you faith in God,
he will show you the why.
The why is simple,
it's all a big test.
Put your trust in him,
he will show you the rest!

***

Your Truth

You know the truth
when all you see,
is people lying
to you and to me.
You value honesty,
respect and trust,
but all you get
is let down and disgust.
So value those
who truly care,
those that are true to you
and want to share.
God knows the heart,
he knows the way.
Make a new start,
start a new day.

***

Be Yourself

Be yourself,
it's who you are.
God created you this way,
you are a rising star.
Stay positive and true
to your inner core.
Don't dwell on your past,
don't close the door.
A new door will open,
to a better you,
and you will be proud
of what you can do!

***

Your Heart

When you give your heart
don't worry about what will be,
or what you start.
You give it freely
for the most part.
You love and you share,
you give and you care.
It may come back,
and it may stop.
But give freely
until your last drop.
You never know
what day will be last,
so give all your heart
until God brings to pass.

***

STEVE RAGGIO

Life is Hard

We try our best,
we worry, we struggle
with each and every test.
We lose loved ones and friends
each and every day,
and through it all,
all we need to do is pray.
Pray for those sickly,
pray for those in need,
say a good word,
do a great deed.
Love all with all your heart,
and if we do that,
we can make a new start.

***

Life is Hard

We try our best,
we worry, we struggle
with each and every test.
We lose loved ones and friends
each and every day,
and through it all,
all we need to do is pray.
Pray for those sickly,
pray for those in need,
say a good word,
do a great deed.
Love all with all your heart,
and if we do that,
we can make a new start.

***

Time

Time is a treasure
that most cannot find,
too busy looking
for what is behind.
Value your minutes,
your days and your weeks.
Enjoy the valleys,
the hills and the peaks.
Count every second
like it may be your last.
Because you never know
what will come to pass.
God only knows
the time and the how,
so live your life
for here and for now!

***

Humble

Be humble,
have thirst
to be last
and not first.
Don't brag
and don't boast
of who has the most.
Some have little
and some have it all.
But money only measures
those that may fall.
Enjoy simple things
that God gives you free.
They're here for you
and they're here for me.

***

Healing

You lay in bed
look at the ceiling.
You're searching
for some sort of healing.
You know your heart,
you know what you're feeling.
Your mind is confused,
your thoughts are reeling.
Who to turn to,
who really cares,
the one that does
is the one that shares.
He shares his love,
his compassion and his grace.
You cannot see him
or touch his face.
But he's there for you
if you allow him to be.
Just let him in
and he will let you see.
The value of life
for you and for me,
Jesus is there
in your time of need.
If you just let him
plant the seed.

***

HEART TALKING

Calling

You don't know your calling,
your path
or your voice.
You ask God
for wisdom,
for clarity of choice.
He will show you
if you follow
his words
and his deeds,
and provide you
with all of your needs.
Don't rely on you
or your mind,
he will teach you
to be true,
to be kind.
Your calling is there
for you to embrace,
until one day
we may see his face.

***

Sunrise

The street lights are on.
The birds in the air,
they're flying and chirping
without any care.
The sun is afar
it's making its way,
to come up and show you
a beautiful day.
So value it's light
it's peace and it's love.
The sunrise is here
from him up above.

***

STEVE RAGGIO

Appreciate

Appreciate the little things,
a walk in the park,
a ride until dark,
a bird flying high,
a beautiful sky,
a cruise on a boat,
a poem that you wrote,
a prayer in your head,
a comfortable bed,
a painting on the wall,
an infant that can crawl
an eye that can see,
a leg and a knee.
It's all about love
and not about hate,
it's what do you appreciate!

***

Sight

Sight is a treasure,
hearing too,
imagine darkness always
and no sounds for you.
So cherish what you see,
the birds and the bees,
the leaves and the trees.
The beach and sun,
the sound of the waves.
Enjoy the beauty
all of your days.
Thanking him above
with all of your soul,
because some cannot see
and still they feel whole.

***

STEVE RAGGIO

Your Worth

You know your worth,
you show it every day.
Some people value it
and some throw it away.
Your worth is valuable
to those who know you best.
Others may doubt it
and put you to the test.
Don't let it get to you
or let it bring you down.
God knows your worth
and will always be around.

***

Your Walk

Walk in truth,
your path is light.
Shine in life
to make things bright.
Walk with courage
to make others see
your inner soul
and who you can be.
Your walk will take you
through heartaches and tears,
through challenges
to face all your fears.
So walk with compassion,
with joy and with love.
Walk with thanks
from our God up above.

***

Words

Words are easy,
they come out clear,
or maybe not,
it's what you hear.
You may hear truth
or you may hear lies.
You may hear joy
or you may hear cries.
Value the words
that speak to your heart.
Start a new day,
make a new start!

***

I Gave My All

I gave my all,
I tried my best.
I put all things
to the test.
I loved a lot
with all my heart.
Didn't realize
would come a new start.
God has a plan
for me I know.
It's all my will
where I should go.
I hope it's where
he wants me to be.
A special place
for me to see.
We cannot judge
or question our way.
He leads us and shows
each and every day.
It may not be
what you think is best.
But he will definitely
show you your test.
And in the end
you will see.
He will guide us,
both you and me!

***

A Kind Word

Everyone needs a kind word.
   They may struggle,
   they may fall,
   they may conquer
   through it all.
   But the kind word
   may get us through.
   A hurtful time,
   for me or for you.
   The words are special
   and true to the heart,
   can start a new day
   and make a new start!

***

We All Live

We all live,
we all will die.
We all will laugh,
we all will cry.
So live your life
with compassion and joy.
For those around you,
the girl and the boy.
The baby, the mother,
the son and daughter,
the friend and the father.
If we value the life
and how we must live.
It's not about us,
it's how we must give.
So don't be greedy
and surely don't boast.
It's how we all live
and who gives the most!

***

Heartbreak

Heartbreak is hard,
it stings to the core.
You thought it was forever,
but now never more.
You gave your heart
all of yourself.
You ask for forgiveness,
you ask for a new start.
Only God knows
what's meant for your soul.
Only God knows
the means and the goal.
You gave your heart
to someone with love.
You asked for blessings,
from high up above.
It didn't work out,
it hurt to the core.
But God is gentle
and he opens a new door.
So don't contemplate,
the sorry and sad.
Just be happy,
for the good and the glad!

***

I'm Sorry

I'm sorry
for what I should do.
For what I should have said,
for what I should have knew.
Didn't know what was meant,
didn't know what was sent.
Did something wrong,
said something right.
May have been good tomorrow,
may have been good tonight.
It's not what was said,
it's not what was done.
It's all about laughter,
it's all about fun.
So don't take things hard,
and don't shed a tear.
Don't carry burdens,
and do not fear.
I'm sorry you cried,
I'm sorry you hurt.
I tried my best,
to value your worth.
In the end please forgive me,
as we know that God will.
I ask for his peace,
his grace and his will!

***

STEVE RAGGIO

Smile

Smile,
it's easy to do.
It benefits me,
and it benefits you.
We all carry burdens,
we all carry tears.
A smile will help you
calm all your fears.
A smile in the morning,
a smile at night.
Makes things special,
makes things bright.
We may be here a little,
we may be here a while.
So brighten one's day
with a beautiful smile!

***

You Tried

You tried your best,
you put your feelings
to the test.
You loved and gave your heart,
gave your all
from the start.
Things didn't work,
it's not all you.
You got to remember
it takes two.
A new path is here
for you to embrace.
A welcome smile
to put on your face.
Put it in God's hands,
he will show your way,
to count your blessings
and start a new day!

***

Love Life

Love life
that's all there is.
It's special,
it's like a quiz.
You ask for something,
for peace and for love,
you ask for forgiveness,
for joy
from above.
If only you would love
what God freely gives,
you would see
how truly he lives.
He lives in your heart,
he lives in your soul,
so loving others
should be your only goal.
Love life for you
and love life for me,
love life for all
so everyone can see!

***

STEVE RAGGIO

I Love Pictures

I love pictures,
I love the past.
It shows where we are going,
it shows what can last.
What can be
and what could.
What may have happened
and what should.
We never know
what pictures we take.
May be forever
or may be too late.
But cherish those pictures,
cause they showed you a time.
Where things were special,
they resembled a rhyme.
They showed you
a special,
and cherished time.
Where things were going,
and things were in line.
So live with your heart,
make a new start.
Make a new friend,
till life comes to an end!

***

HEART TALKING

STEVE RAGGIO

Judge Me

Judge me
if you may.
Your words
have nothing to say.
God knows my heart,
he knows my mind,
he knows my faith,
he knows I'm kind.
I have faults,
everyone does,
it's what's here
and not what was.
I want to live
to be my best,
to show God
and pass the test.
The test is love
to show it all,
and God will bless me
and not let me fall!

***

Give Thanks

Give thanks
to God up above,
who shows us his mercy
and all of his love.
I'm thankful for blessings
he gives me each day,
the freedom to live,
the freedom to pray.
I'm thankful for health,
for family and friends,
the faith that God wants
the joy that he sends.
I'm thankful for the soldier
who died so that we
can live a happy life
so we can be free.
So count each day
like it may be your last,
value the simple things,
don't dwell on the past!

***

STEVE RAGGIO

I'm Not Perfect

I'm not perfect,
don't tread on me,
trying to be better
than I used to be.
I may falter,
I may stumble,
I may cry,
I may crumble.
I will try
to be my best,
but please
don't put me to the test.
I work on me,
you work on you,
in the end
we will see,
what we can do!

***

Peace

Peace is needed
in every way,
it gives you comfort
to start a new day.
Peace is a blessing
that you have in your life,
to battle your fears
and fight all the strife.
It's not always easy
to find that true peace,
but when you do
your value will increase.
So ask God to guide you,
to send you your peace,
and blessings will come
and worry will cease!

***

STEVE RAGGIO

Wisdom

We all need wisdom
a clear eye to see,
what God wants for you,
what God wants for me.
The wisdom to learn,
the wisdom to grow,
the wisdom to search,
the wisdom to know.
To know is to give,
to give is to love,
for all around you
and God up above!

***

Have Compassion

Have compassion,
have a kind heart,
forgive someone,
make a new start.
Think of another
as God would want you to,
to bless their soul
through and through.
Someone is hurting,
going through pain,
just listen to them
in the end you will gain.
Gain not the sympathy,
gain not the star,
look within,
look not afar.
They are looking for love,
for simple and kind,
for something special,
for some peace of mind.
So allow them to think
to be who they are,
to shine their light,
like a shining star!

***

A Lie

A lie is a lie,
it's definitely not true.
It only hurts me,
it doesn't hurt you.
You lie to my face
and think I don't see,
the truth is not there
or what it should be.
Truth is special,
it comes from the soul.
A lie is deceiving
it creates a new hole.
The hurt that it causes
to loved ones and me,
causes a wedge
for everyone to see.
A lie is not good
it's not what God shows.
The truth is special
it loves and it grows!

***

Love

Love is faithful,
love is kind.
Love is endearing,
love is not blind.
Love sees you through
each and every day.
To follow you path,
to show you your way.
So embrace this day
with love in your heart.
Show them the way,
make a new start!

***

I'm Going

I'm going on an excursion,
I'm going on a ride.
Don't expect you to come,
or be by my side.
I'm going just for me
to figure things out.
To live and laugh,
to sing and to shout.
I'm going just to see
where my story goes.
And who I can be
where nobody knows.
I can be special
or I can be to blame.
I can be valuable
or one to cause to shame.
I'm going to take the road
that shows me the way.
To start a new path,
to brighten someone's day!

***

A New Year

A new year is here,
for you to embrace,
with joy and with love
and a smile on your face.
Shed all your fear,
your doubt and your worry,
take life slowly
without any hurry.
The race is not
a sprint to the end,
make someone happy,
make a new friend.
Friends are special,
they make it clear,
to love and cherish,
to start a new year!

***

Sometime

Sometime it's now,
sometime forever.
Sometime wow,
sometimes never.
Sometime a little,
sometime a bunch.
Sometime for dinner,
sometime for lunch.
Sometime for good,
sometime for sad.
Sometime for happy,
sometime for glad.
Sometime for me,
sometime fo you.
Spend some time with God
see what he can do!

***

I Don't Know

I don't know the why,
I don't know the when,
I don't know the beginning,
I don't know the end.
I don't know who's right,
I don't know who's wrong,
I don't know it all,
I don't know it all along.
I don't know the answers,
I don't know the test,
I don't know the questions,
I don't know the rest.
I don't know the way
he wants me to go,
but please show me, God
I want to know.

***

Be a Beacon

Be a beacon
a light that shines,
a light that's true,
a light that's kind.
Shine your light
for all to see,
what I mean to you
and you to me.
Your light is a blessing
from God up above
to shine upon all
and show them your love.
The beacon of light,
that's in your heart,
can brighten one's day
and make a new start!

***

Negativity

Negativity is a weight
that brings you down,
it's not healthy,
can make you frown.
Some people bring it,
it gets in your way
to follow your path
to start a new day.
So concentrate on good,
positive thoughts and all.
Sometimes you may stumble,
sometimes you may fall.
Pick yourself up
to bring life your best,
God will help you
and show you the rest!

***

Friends

Friends are special,
the ones that are true.
They are here for me
and they are here for you.
You know the true ones
that are here since your past,
and not so true ones
that you know just won't last.
So cherish the ones
that bring joy to your life,
not the ones
that only brings strife.
God sends us friends
to love in all ways,
so show them your love
till our final days!

***

I Search

I search,
I try to find.
True happiness,
true peace of mind.
It comes in time,
true friends show their love.
And blessings flow
from God up above.
Times that we treasure,
times that are unfair.
Value each day
with love and with care.
But through the pain,
the loss and the hurt.
There is light in the end
that will change your worth.
Your worth is there
so value it each day.
To shine your light
and show them your way!

***

STEVE RAGGIO

Friends are Special

Friends are special,
they bring joy to your life.
They show you your path
and help you with strife.
Show them your heart
and lead them the way,
to bless others
in a start of a new day.
True friends will be there
when you're down and out,
when you're at your best
they will jump and shout.
So cherish your friends
and show them your love,
and blessings will flow
from God up above!

***

I Don't Know

I don't know the future
I don't know the why
I don't know tomorrow
or what's in the sky.
The sky is here
for all to see,
for God's blessings
for you
and for me.
So take in that beauty
and cherish the look
God gives you that
and also his book!

***

STEVE RAGGIO

I Have Hurt

I have hurt in my heart,
I feel the pain.
I ask for his mercy,
to heal my shame.
His mercy is great,
his love is all,
I know I stumble,
I know I fall.
But I pick myself up
and look for the day
that we all will love
each other as we pray!

***

I Live My Life

I live my life,
I try to find
true happiness,
true peace of mind.
It's hard sometimes,
I may care too much
for others feelings
and their wants and such.
Sometimes I feel guilty
for tending to my needs,
for feeling loving
or doing small deeds.
I just ask God for help,
for showing the way
to cope with things
and start a new day!

***

I Don't Know the Why

I don't know the why,
I don't know the way,
only he knows
our path each day.
I don't know my future
but give it to him,
allow him to work,
in the end I will win.
I follow the road
the path that he makes,
I know it's right
for goodness sake's.
My path is damaged
with fear and with shame,
but his path is true
with truth and no pain!

***

I Look For Clarity

I look for clarity
in my thoughts and deeds.
I look for guidance
in my wants and needs.
The clarity can come
if I don't rely on me.
Rely on God
to make me see,
make me see the path
you want me to take,
to grow and to love,
to mold and to make.
I know I'm human,
I stumble and I fall,
have mercy on me
and mercy on us all!

***

STEVE RAGGIO

You Give Your All

You give your all,
you think it's true,
you think forever,
you think me and you.
You love each other
you think it's right,
But it hurts your heart
because you know it's not right.
Right is simple,
it;s peace and it's love,
it's not chaos,
it comes from above.
He teaches patience,
he teaches kind,
he wants you to love
To soothe your mind.
Your mind is special,
he wants you to feel
what is for you
and what is truly real!

***

I'm Trying

I'm trying,
I'm trying to find
true clarity,
true peace of mind.
I'm trying to be
a beacon of light
to shine on others,
to make things bright.
I know I'm not perfect
a work in progress,
to care for others
and share with the less.
So as I try to be
better than before
please show me the way God,
please open the door!

***

The Birds

The birds are chirping,
it's in the air,
flying around
like they just don't care.
Looks like no worries
going about their life,
living peacefully
with little or no strife.
I guess the chirping
is sharing their love
for each other
and from God up above!

***

You May Like Me

You may like me,
you may not.
You may ridicule me
on the spot.
But I am loved,
I know it's true,
it's a gift from God
for me and you.
Accept his grace
his love and care
so you can give
and you can share.
Share your love
you have in your heart
to make someone happy
and create a new start!

***

Disrespect

Disrespect is there
it hurts your heart.
You know your truth
right from the start.
You know that you seek
compassion and love.
Your true blessings
from God up above.
When disrespect comes
from someone close.
Focus on yourself
and things you value most.
If someone doesn't respect you
don't take it to heart.
You know who you are,
make a new start!

***

I Want a Love

I want a love
that you share your all
with someone that loves you
and makes you stand tall.
A love that is peaceful,
a love that is kind
a love that is giving
all of the time.
That love is special,
it comes from the heart
to warm your soul
and make a new start!

***

STEVE RAGGIO

My Heart is Heavy

My heart is heavy,
my smile hides the hurt.
I try to be happy
and value my worth.
Sometimes I doubt it
but God has my back.
I put trust in him
for things I may lack.
I'm getting better
each and every day
with his help
as I sit here and pray.
He leads me on
to a path that's true
for a better me
and a better you!

***

I'm Searching

I'm searching,
searching to find
some sort of peace,
some sort of kind.
I'm searching within,
which leaves me without
the truth that comes
with worry and doubt.
If I would only search
for his love and grace
God will put
a smile on my face!

***

A New Day

The sun is rising
to start a new day.
Be thankful and joyful
as we reflect and we pray.
Reflect on the good
not thinking of the bad.
Reflect on the happy
and not on the sad.
The sad can come,
it's part of life
but dwell on it too long
will cause you more strife.
Cast your worries to God,
he will show you the way
to follow his path
and start a new day!

***

Disrespect II

Disrespect is bad,
it takes you away
to another place
that's far away.
It bothers your soul
it hurts to the core,
takes away your joy
knocks you to the floor.
If you can't respect someone
then your compass is wrong,
treat those with respect
and make them belong!

***

Trust

Trust is everything,
it's what we need.
If you can't trust them
you can't proceed.
Broken trust
hurts your heart
causes division,
tears you apart.
So value yourself,
trust in your heart
to start a new day
and make a new start!

***

You May Be

You may be in my life a little,
you may be in my life a while.
If it's just a little
and not a while
let's be happy
and end it with a smile!

***

STEVE RAGGIO

In This Life

In this life,
if it's on your mind
and it's truly kind,
share it
Or it's left behind!

***

A Beautiful Day

A beautiful day,
be thankful for that,
always a blessing
wherever you're at.
Go for a walk,
take in a ride,
spend it with loved ones
right by your side.
It's the simple things
that brings us a smile.
So live for the moment
and live for the while!

***

Memorial Day

Memorial Day,
a time to listen,
a time to pray.
It's what they did
that means a lot
to have our freedom
and what we've got.
The ultimate sacrifice
is what they give,
so we can be
and we can live.
Live with thanks,
blessing to be,
they gave their life
so we would be free!

***

Take It Slow

Take it slow.
Let guidance
from up above,
show you where to go.
Let his peace
flow in
like a rolling tide.
Don't hurry,
just enjoy the ride.
Enjoy the good
don't fret over bad.
Cherish the happy,
don't dwell on the sad.
Good things will come,
just wait and see.
Blessings will flow
through you
and through me!

***

STEVE RAGGIO

The Sun is Rising

The sun is rising,
a beautiful sight.
God's creation
to shine his light.
To start a new day,
be thankful for that.
Wherever you go,
wherever you're at.
It's the simple things
that should bring us joy.
A baby's smile
playing with a toy.
So start your day
with joy in your heart.
Make someone happy
make a new start!

***

I Don't Know Why

I don't know why,
I don't know the reason,
God show me the way,
show me the season.
Make it easy
for me to see
my love for others
your love for me.
Show me how to give
with a kind heart
to bless others
with a new start.
A new start is good,
it fills a hole
with blessings from above
to feed your soul!

***

Cherish Your Loved Ones

Cherish your loved ones
we don't know the time,
I may have 100 new poems
or just one more rhyme.
Give them your presence,
give them your love
blessings will flow
from God up above.
It's the simple things
that bring us much joy,
the first words of a baby
the girl and the boy.
So love deeply
With passion in your soul
a smile on someone's face
should be your ultimate goal!

***

I'm Not Perfect

I'm not perfect,
never said I was,
everyone has faults,
everyone does.
You stumble,
you fall
God still loves you
through it all.
But don't condemn you
and don't condemn me,
in the end
you will see,
if you give it to God
in his presence you will be!

***

Cancer

Cancer is cruel,
cancer is mean.
Eats at your body,
very unclean.
Takes away loved ones,
causes much pain.
For those that have it
you hardly hear complain.
Tests your faith,
pulls at your core.
Creates a path
to open a new door.
Some will suffer more,
some will suffer less.
But Jesus suffered the most
when they put him to the test.
Nailed to the cross,
spit in his face.
So if we give it to him
we have a better place.
He says to cast your worries
on him you will see.
He has a better place
for you and for me!

***

A Beautiful Morning

A beautiful morning
for all to see
comes from above
for you and for me.
Take it in,
be thankful for that
wherever you are
wherever you're at.
Listen to the birds
all different in sound,
just loving life,
just hanging around.
If we could mirror them
that comes from above,
this world would be better
with peace and with love!

***

STEVE RAGGIO

Give Your Love

Give your love
it may come back
or maybe not,
as a matter of fact.
But if you give your love
with a kind heart
it may bless someone
to make a new start,
to put away bitterness,
to ease someone's pain,
bring joy to their life,
bring sunshine not rain.
Say a kind word,
do a good deed,
may provide some joy
for someone in need!

***

I Sit Here and Ponder

I sit here and ponder,
what this day will bring.
As the sun comes up
and the birds sing.
Their sound is music,
each one a different note.
You know it's special,
it's what God wrote.
He wrote the tunes
for us to hear.
To show love to others,
to bring others near.
Near to our heart
and near to our soul.
So we can be joyful
and we can be whole!

***

Look For the Good

Look for the good,
not at the bad.
Look for the happy,
not at the sad.
It's easy to look
for fault and for shame,
look for the good
in all those we love.
Look for the good
from God up above.
The good is there
for all to behold,
the good to shape us,
to create a new mold.
Mold us to be
a reflection of you
to create a new start,
to start a new you!

***

I May Live

I may live till morning,
I may live a while,
I may go a minute,
I may go a mile.
It's not the endurance,
it's not just the test,
it's how we love
not who's the best.
So live your life fully,
give till it hurts,
show someone compassion,
show someone your worth.
Your life is not a picture
of what someone can see,
it's just a symbol
of what someone can be!

***

STEVE RAGGIO

The Beauty

The beauty on the outside
only goes so far,
diminishes with aging
Like tires on a car.
The beauty on the inside
shows who you are,
so let it shine
around you and afar.
Brighten one's day
with a word that is kind,
a beautiful smile
to ease someone's mind.
The beauty is not
what all can see,
the beauty is
what all can be.
So let your inner beauty
light up a day,
make someone happy,
show them the way!

***

The Path

Do you know the path
that you should take
in the morning
when you awake?
The path of love,
the path of hate,
the path of early,
the path of late.
The path of happy,
the path of sad,
the path of friendly,
the path of mad.
The path of joy,
the path of gloom,
the path of righteousness,
the path of doom.
You can choose the path
and choose to be,
the path of love
for all to see.

***

Three

Family and Friends and the Soul

Brady Charles

Brady Charles loves his music,
his golf and his buds.
Makes a few birdies
but makes a few duds.
A loyal friend,
to those in his core.
Loves his family,
that's for sure.
I'm proud of him,
of where he may go.
Write a new song,
start a new show.
Whatever you do,
happy or sad.
I'm here for you
cause I'm your dad!
(Love you!)

***

Gabby

Gabby is my daughter
true to the core.
But don't cross her
she will show you the door.
A giving heart,
for all to see.
A beautiful person
as anyone could be.
She will give her last dollar
to those who may lack.
Will give you her heart,
the shirt off her back.
Proud of her
through happy and sad.
Knowing well
that I am her dad!
(Love you!)

***

Miss Lauren

Miss Lauren
it's plain to see.
You're a beautiful person
as anyone could be.
My youngest daughter,
a giving heart.
Ever looking,
to make a new start.
A beautiful soul
that shines through the dark.
Always looking
to make a new mark.
Her light will shine
for all to see.
Makes me proud
cause I'm her daddy!
(Love you!)

***

Allie Girl

Allie Girl my daughter,
it's plain to see.
You came from your mother
and not from me.
They call me your step,
but that's not how I feel.
You're my daughter
and that's for real.
A beautiful heart,
for all to see.
Full of giving
to all and to me.
You will go far in life,
I know that to be.
So shine your light
for all to see.
(Love you!)

***

My Dad

My dad would say
we have a something,
a thing in common,
the same birthday.
A humble man
never one to boast,
never one to brag
or one for a toast.
Had a simple way
to show you he cared,
and a beautiful soul
that he welcomely shared.
Loved his wife
his kids and his friends,
and was brutally honest
every day till the end.
Learned a lot from him
but one thing stood clear,
love with your heart
and love with no fear!
(Love you!)

***

My Mom

My mom was hard
but loving too.
Let you know how she felt
and what you need to do.
Her nickname was Red,
and gave you that look.
And you knew
that's all that it took.
She loved us all
and my dad too.
Was there when we needed,
what good moms do!
(Love you!)

***

My Brother

I lost my brother,
a beautiful soul.
A loving man,
a heart of gold.
Would give anything
to one that is need.
Never to slow
to do a good deed.
Slow to anger,
quick to listen.
A beautiful heart
that was sure to glisten.
Gone too soon
but will always remember.
He passed two days before
Jesus' birthday in December!
(Love you!)

***

STEVE RAGGIO

My Sister

My sister is nice,
loyal to those close.
Very protective
her family the most.
Never one to shy
from telling her mind.
Tells it like it is
not leaving things behind.
Takes after Mom
in having a say.
What's on her mind
each and every day.
She loves her family
that's for sure.
If you cross her,
she will show you the door!
(Love you Sis!)

***

My Brother Nerv

My brother Nerv,
a heart of gold.
Always giving
need not be told.
Loves his wife,
his dog too.
His family and friends
a bourbon or a few.
We have a great bond,
I know that to be.
He's a great man,
he's there for me.
(Love you Brother!)

***

I Lost a Bud

I lost a bud,
as happy as can be.
Who had an accident
could've happened to me.
Lost his walking,
confined to a chair.
But loved life
without a care.
He had no blame
or animosity to be.
Just loved life
and his whole family.
He is now with his maker,
his God up above.
Sharing his compassion
and all of his love.

***

My Friend

(Garrett O'Connor)

Selfless to a "T,"
my friend would always think about me.
With one friend or two, six maybe eight.
He made everyone feel special,
everyone feel great.
Cooking at their camp
or at Don's sipping a beer.
He was a special man,
always full of cheer.
He always took care of
his friends, his family and his bride.
Never frowning or complaining
but always standing by your side.
I was blessed to know him
and call him my friend.
And will love and miss him
until we shall meet again.

***

Audra

She loves her way.
To bless her travelers
with a special day.
It comes out in her smile,
she makes you comfortable.
Not just a little
but for a good while.
She makes your trip nice,
makes you want to fly.
Not just once
but definitely twice.
Enjoyed the flight,
keep up what you do.
Not just for us
but also for you!

***

Savanna

Savanna Savanna,
a friend to you
a friend to me.
Creating a smile
for all to see.
Loving her pour
a drink or two.
Creating memories
for one
or a few.
It's very special
to not see her boast.
She makes you a drink,
you thank her
with a toast!

***

STEVE RAGGIO

Pinball Junkies

You go to the zoo
to see some monkeys.
I've got some friends,
some pinball junkies.
Kelly and Craig
love to see
a pinball machine
and some company.
Pinball in the morning,
pinball at night,
pinball out of town,
pinball out of sight.
They love their friends
but don't get in their way.
Cause pinball is special
each and every day.
Craig loves to cook
and his food is good.
But pinball comes first
as we know it should.
If Kelly beats him
on a machine that he built.
It's game on
cause Craig is on tilt!

***

The River Rats

The River Rats are coming
to the river today.
You got Mrs. Pam
and Mr. Balakay.
You got Mayor Cliff
and Aimee too.
You got Lynn
and then you got Drew.
You got Stevo
times two.
You got Claudia
and a few.
You got Ryan
and Kelly times two.
You got Craig
who would ever knew.
Such a fine group
who has a blast.
Let's toast to the future
and thanks to the past!

***

STEVE RAGGIO

Big Cliff

Big Cliff,
the mayor of False River.
A good friend
always a giver.
Loves Mrs. Aimee,
friends and family too.
Loves something old
and something new.
Loves his boat
cruising the lake.
With friends in tow,
usually until daybreak.
Loves to entertain,
never to lack.
Will share anything,
the shirt off his back.
My neighbor at the lake
a sidewalk that he built.
Bothers my bud Craig
like his pinball on tilt!
Just a little joke
for my bud Big Cliff.
A toast to you,
make sure it's not too stiff!

***

They Call Me Bruce

They call me Bruce,
a good friend I know.
Loves his karate
and his dojo.
Mostly quiet,
not one to boast.
But is usually ready
if you want to make a toast.
Loves his bay
with a little St. Louis.
Cruising on his pontoon
with friends that are ruleless.
Mr. Seven Eleven
on Tuesday morn.
But makes his appearance
like the red on a barn.
A toast to my friend,
a man not obtuse.
A good dude
they call me Bruce!

***

Shakey Loves His Traeger

Shakey loves his Traeger
it's how he likes to grill.
Puts the bong down
gets himself a thrill.
Gummies last so long
a drink in hand.
He lights that Traeger,
plays the music of the band.
Puts the wings
straight on the pit.
Scratches his butt
until the pit is lit.
Eats a little brownie
drinks a little sip.
Loves that Traeger grill,
thinks he's hip.
Shakey loves his Traeger grill
till dusk and dawn.
Shakey loves it
on the back of his lawn.

***

Terapy Girl Terapy Boy

Terapy girl,
Terapy boy.
Drink till morning
play with toy.
Always tore up,
always lit.
Can't get up
can't fit.
Need some terapy,
need some rest.
Need a terapist
a medicine chest.
Try to help
but just can't.
They need meetings
or just to rant.
It's all liquor,
and it ain't cheap.
It's really simple
they need some sleep!

***

STEVE RAGGIO

Teddy and Scottie

Teddy and Scottie
a team in the ropes.
Not only for golf
but to create new hopes.
Hopes for better,
for closer to God.
Bringing others along
with a smile and a nod.
It's not just the winning,
it's who they portray.
To lead others to him,
to start a new day!

***

Addison and Maddison

Addison and Maddison,
friends to the core.
One likes to read
one likes outdoor.
Both are super nice,
outgoing and all.
Read a little book
or walk and not fall.
Both are in the bars
taking care of others.
Looking after each other
following their lucky stars.
Here's to the two
happy, happy friends.
Together now
and together to the ends!

***

STEVE RAGGIO

A Great Group

A great group
of close friends.
We all have a blast
till the night ends.
You got Newsmax
who knows everything.
You got Lisa
who likes to sing.
You got Bruce,
loves his dojo.
You got Stitch
the sewing hoe.
You got Charlie
who dances till dawn.
You got Shakey
with a Traeger on his lawn.
You got Hoochie
always in the loop.
You got Critty,
always has the scoop.
You got my brother Nerv
who is surely a trip.
You got Laurie
she only wants a sip.
You got Lush,
he drinks all the time.
You got Nervman,
he likes a little rhyme.
You got Sherideth,

a great hostess.
You got Bae,
she loves her wine the mostess.
You got Gadget
who likes to fix a thing.
I'm thankful for this group
and all that they bring!

**

TD and Stitch

TD loves to dance
and is very able.
But likes to make his moves
on the kitchen table.
Stitch likes to sew
and make a piece of clothes.
Charlie likes to call them
the stitching hoes.
The stitching bitches
has a certain ring.
It's what she likes to do
I guess it is her thing.
Charlie sells a house,
maybe a car or two.
It's what he likes to do.
I like our group
and hanging out with you.
A great friendship,
here's to both of you!

***

My Friend Mason

My friend Mason,
a beautiful soul.
If you ever meet him
his heart is like gold.
His smile is true,
it comes from the heart.
His love for his friends
shows from the start.
He loves his Vaqueros,
his kids and his wife.
I'm blessed with his friendship
and a part of his life!
(RIP amigo)

***

STEVE RAGGIO

Tejas Vaqueros

Tejas Vaqueros mean to me
a special bond
for all to see.
It's not about status,
it's not just the ride,
I know my brothers are with me,
and stand by my side.
They are with you
through good times and bad,
will be there for you
if you are happy or sad.
The music is special,
The ride is great
I count on my brothers
if I'm early or if I'm late.
We toast to each other
and laugh a bunch,
no matter just hanging
or eating some lunch.
I value this bond
And know that it's pure
and hope for mi amigos
that I see them next year!

***

The Blessings of a Child

The blessings of a child
for all to see.
It's special for you and for me.
God gives us this gift
to cherish,
and to behold.
It's like fine wine,
it's like pure gold.
The unconditional love
God gives us to see.
Shines through a young child
for you and for me.
So cherish the birth,
the cries and the paths.
The blessings they give,
the smiles and the laughs!

***

The Joy

The joy of a child
a beautiful thing.
Their love is pure,
the comfort that they bring.
Those little words
they speak each day.
Bring a smile to your face
in every way.
Their joy is a blessing
from God up above.
He shows us that
through a child's love!

***

Big Nasty

Big Nasty is pretty,
Big Nasty is sweet.
Doesn't know how she touches
people she meets.
Her kindness is great,
it shows on her face.
Every time I see her
in every place.
Thanks Big Nasty
for all that you bring.
Joy to people's lives,
be happy and sing!

***

STEVE RAGGIO

My Buddy Gil

My buddy Gil,
kind to the core.
Will give of himself
and a whole lot more.
Was a major league pitcher,
a good golfer too.
A father and friend
to name a few.
But the thing that I value,
truly the most.
Is our friendship
and he's a pretty good host!
(Love you, man!)

***

Brothers Guidry

Brothers Guidry
You got Danny,
You got Eddie
and Gary too.
All like my brothers
to name a few.
No matter what day,
no matter what time.
I can count on each
at the drop of a dime.
True friends to me
and even more.
Like adopted brothers
love them to the core!

***

My Bud

My bud was a good man,
always smiling from ear to ear.
Never worried about much,
never carrying much fear.
He watched his Andy Griffith,
he drank his Coors Light.
He loved hanging with his buds from morning until night.
He wasn't worried about money,
fancy cars or material things.
No designer clothes,
no bling bling rings.
He worried more about his friends,
was loyal to the core.
And if you were one of his buds you knew it for sure.
He will be missed by all and especially by me.
So long my friend
until again we shall meet!

***

HEART TALKING

Acknowledgements

I have to thank God foremost for giving me the blessings to write these poems. Though a lot of them may be simple they truly came from my heart! Want to thank David Jahr for helping me put together this book and my Vaquero brother Mike Kohler for introducing us. Want to also thank my family and friends for their support! You all mean a bunch to me!
   Love y'all!

About the Author

It's all good! That's one of our favorite sayings at my business. Sometimes it may be all good and sometimes not. But I try to look for the positive in everything. I am a businessman that has a successful business for 39 years. I am a proud father and grandfather. I have friends and family that truly bless my life. I am recently divorced and through my alone time and healing I started writing poems. It truly helped me and through Gods blessings I have compiled them into this book. I hope they can bring some inspiration to my readers and bring them closer to God as it has made me closer to him through writing them! I was born, raised and still live in "Cajun Country" of Lafayette, Louisiana.

God Bless,

Steve

www.ingramcontent.com/pod-product-compliance
Lightning Source LLC
LaVergne TN
LVHW012018060526
838201LV00061B/4362